A KID'S GUIDE TO FEELINGS

FEELING
EMBARRASSED

BY KIRSTY HOLMES

KidHaven
PUBLISHING

Published in 2019 by KidHaven Publishing, an Imprint of Greenhaven Publishing, LLC
353 3rd Avenue, Suite 255, New York, NY 10010

Written by: Kirsty Holmes
Edited by: John Wood
Designed by: Danielle Rippengill

Cataloging-in-Publication Data

Names: Holmes, Kirsty.
Title: Feeling embarrassed / Kirsty Holmes.
Description: New York : KidHaven Publishing, 2019. | Series: A kid's guide to feelings | Includes glossary and index.
Identifiers: ISBN 9781534527003 (pbk.) | ISBN 9781534526990 (library bound) | ISBN 9781534527010 (6 pack)
Subjects: LCSH: Embarrassment in children--Juvenile literature. | Embarrassment--Juvenile literature. | Emotions--Juvenile literature.
Classification: LCC BF723.E44 H645 2019 | DDC 152.4'4--dc23

*All images are courtesy of Shutterstock.com, unless otherwise specified. With thanks to Getty Images,
Thinkstock Photo and iStockphoto.* Front Cover – MarinaMay, yayasya, jirawat phueksriphan, Piotr Urakau,
Kate Aedon, anna.danilkova, Rawpixel.com. Images used on every page – MarinaMay, yayasya, Piotr Urakau.
4 – jirawat phueksriphan. 5&6 – Elegant Solution, Oxy_gen. 7 – YoPixArt. 8 – Aleksandr Sementinov, Africa Studio.
9 – Melody A, Ganis, Africa Studio. 11 – Littlekidmoment, Warut Chinsai, Twin Design. 12 – Rawpixel.com, Evellean,
cristovao. 13 – Evellean, backUp. 14 – Glinskaja Olga, wisnukrist, YoPixArt. 15 – Marcos Mesa Sam Wordley, kitty,
Fotos593. 16 – VaLiza. 17 – Veronica Louro. 18 – Asier Romero. 19 – YoPixArt. 21 – Ana Blazic Pavlovic, Oxy_gen,
kearia, Marina R. 22&23 – Elegant Solution, Oxy_gen, kearia.

Printed in the United States of America

CPSIA compliance information: Batch # BS18KL: For further information contact Greenhaven Publishing LLC, New York, New York at 1-844-317-7404.

CONTENTS

Words that look Like **this** can be found in the glossary on page 24.

We all have **emotions**, or feelings, all the time. Our feelings are very important. They help us think about the world around us, and know how we want to **react**.

Sometimes, we feel good. Other times, we feel bad.

Shrinking Violet is feeling pretty embarrassed.

Let's find out more… 7

HOW DO WE FEEL
WHEN WE'RE EMBARRASSED?

Your face might feel really hot…

...you might have a sinking feeling in your belly...

...you might feel sweaty...

… or you might want to run away, or cry.

8

HOW DO WE LOOK
WHEN WE'RE EMBARRASSED?

WIDE EYES!

RAISED EYEBROWS!

RED CHEEKS!

OPEN MOUTH!

TRYING TO HIDE!

WHY DO WE FEEL EMBARRASSED?

FEELING EMBARRASSED IS AN IMPORTANT EMOTION.

Human beings live together in a **society**.

Societies have different rules...

BE POLITE	☑	
BE NICE	☑	
GO TO SCHOOL	☑	
DON'T PUSH	☑	

12

DON'T TRIP AND FALL!

DON'T CALL THE TEACHER "MOM"

...and all of us learn these rules.

If we get one of these rules wrong, we feel embarrassed.

THINGS THAT
MAKE US EMBARRASSED

WHEN FEELING
EMBARRASSED IS GOOD

Feeling embarrassed can be a good thing. If you and someone else have been embarrassed together, you can laugh about it afterwards.

I CAN'T BELIEVE WE DID THAT!

16

If we have something important to do, we will **prepare** better for it to make sure we aren't embarrassed.

WHEN FEELING EMBARRASSED IS BAD

Feeling embarrassed might make us not want to do something again...

It's important to listen to our feelings of embarrassment.
But don't let it make you sad.

Everyone makes mistakes from time to time!

DEALING WITH FEELINGS

Shrinking Violet needs to laugh about it.

Her friends will help her to feel better. Agents of F.E.E.L.S: GO!

LET'S HELP!

Talking about your feelings can help you to understand why you feel embarrassed.

GLOSSARY

BODY LANGUAGE   things a person does with their body that tell you how they feel

COMPLIMENT   praise someone or something

EMOTIONS   strong feelings such as joy, hate, sadness, or fear

PREPARE   get ready

RAISED   lifted up

REACT   act or respond to something that has been done

SOCIETY   a collection of people living together in a group

STUTTER   find it difficult to speak

INDEX